Little Dove

with scripture to introduce
your child to The Holy Spirit

Third in the JUST LIKE US series

By Marion W. Richardson

Marion W. Richardson
3660 Highway 41
Stanley, New Mexico 87056-9708
www.marionwrichardson.com

ISBN-13: 978-1497372993
ISBN-10: 1497372992
First Edition

All scripture references are to the
King James Version of the Holy Bible.

Forward

The Holy Spirit is found throughout the Bible, both in the Old and New Testaments. His work is acclaimed. His position in the Trinity is undeniable. He, along with God, the Father, and Jesus, the Son, are described as being together at creation and at Jesus' baptism. We are told to "Go ye therefore, and teach all nations, baptizing them in the name of the Father, and of the Son, and of the Holy Ghost." Matthew 28:19.

He is called "the Spirit of The Lord." He seals, anoints, and empowers. The scriptures compare His actions to that of water, wind, fire, oil, wine, and seed. The most frequent and possibly the most recognized symbol for the Spirit is that of a dove. In Matthew 3:16, Jesus emerges from the water "and, lo, the heavens were opened unto him, and he saw the Spirit of God descending like a dove, and lighting upon him."

It is my desire that young children come to recognize the move of the Holy Spirit in their lives. By identifying and illustrating fourteen actions of the little dove, I hope that the character of the Spirit of The Lord is more understandable to both young and old.

May this be just the beginning of your journey with the Spirit of The Lord!

Love,

Marion

Miss Marion

Little Dove is a lot like
the Spirit of The Lord.

Little Dove sings a new song

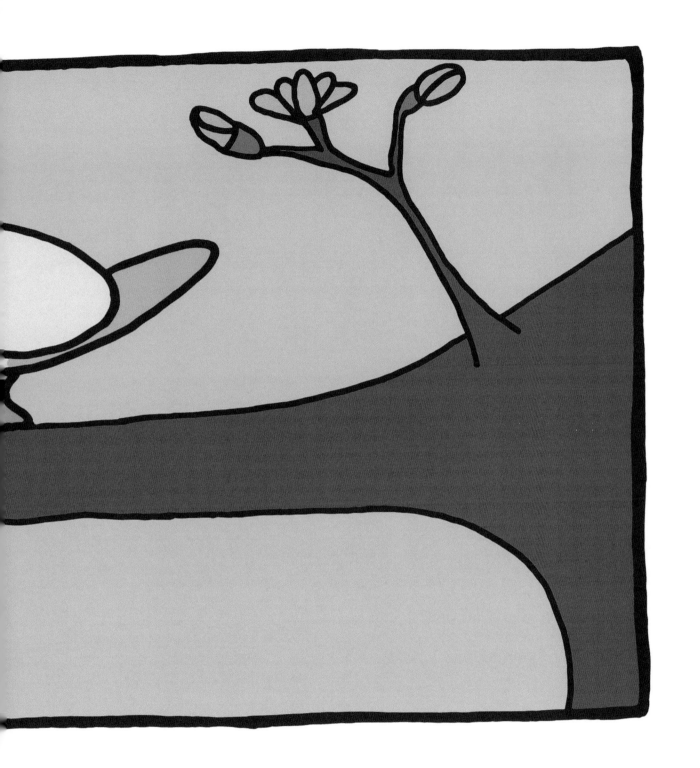

just like the Spirit of The Lord.

Little Dove flutters
over the waters

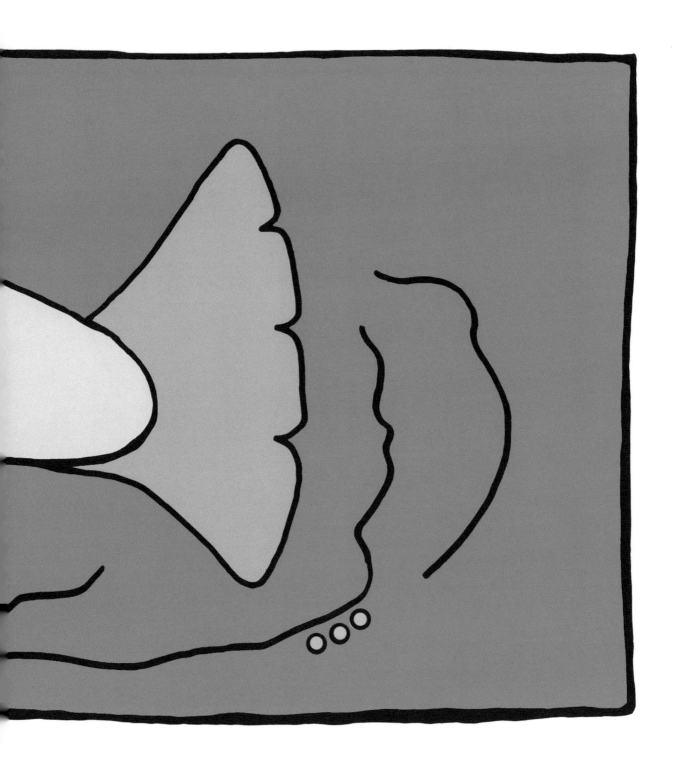

just like the Spirit of The Lord.

Little Dove lights gently

just like the Spirit of The Lord.

Little Dove bathes in the light

just like the Spirit of The Lord.

Little Dove loves deeply

just like the Spirit of The Lord.

Little Dove quenches thirst

just like the Spirit of The Lord.

Little Dove breathes
comforting coos

just like the Spirit of The Lord.

Little Dove leads his flock

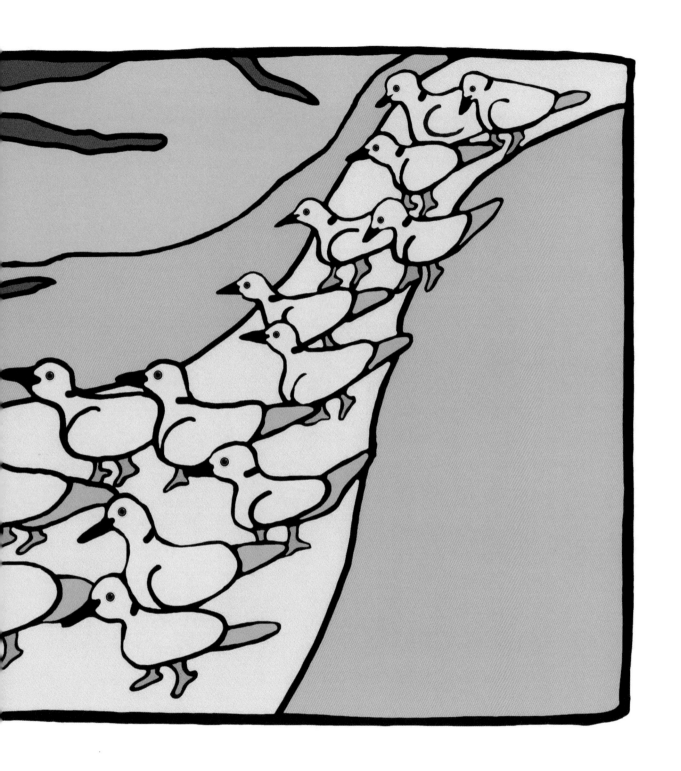

just like the Spirit of The Lord.

Little Dove cries out in warning

just like the Spirit of The Lord.

Little Dove flies
freely and swiftly

just like the Spirit of The Lord.

Little Dove teaches wisdom

just like the Spirit of The Lord.

Little Dove crafts skillfully

just like the Spirit of The Lord.

Little Dove searches
for good grain

just like the Spirit of The Lord.

Little Dove soars
on mighty wings

just like the Spirit of The Lord.

Not many people see the
Spirit of The Lord,

but we see how His
acts change our lives.

KEY SCRIPTURE

John 3:5-8

5 Jesus answered, Verily, verily, I say unto thee, Except a man be born of water and of the Spirit, he cannot enter into the kingdom of God. 6 That which is born of the flesh is flesh; and that which is born of the Spirit is spirit. 7 Marvel not that I said unto thee, Ye must be born again. 8 The wind bloweth where it listeth, and thou hearest the sound thereof, but canst not tell whence it cometh, and whither it goeth: so is every one that is born of the Spirit.

1 Thessalonians 5:16-19

16 Rejoice evermore. 17 Pray without ceasing. 18 In every thing give thanks: for this is the will of God in Christ Jesus concerning you. 19 Quench not the Spirit.

KEY SCRIPTURE

1 Corinthians 12:3-11

3 Wherefore I give you to understand, that no man speaking by the Spirit of God calleth Jesus accursed: and that no man can say that Jesus is the Lord, but by the Holy Ghost. 4 Now there are diversities of gifts, but the same Spirit. 5 And there are differences of administrations, but the same Lord. 6 And there are diversities of operations, but it is the same God which worketh all in all. 7 But the manifestation of the Spirit is given to every man to profit withal. 8 For to one is given by the Spirit the word of wisdom; to another the word of knowledge by the same Spirit; 9   To another faith by the same Spirit; to another the gifts of healing by the same Spirit; 10   To another the working of miracles; to another prophecy; to another discerning of spirits; to another divers kinds of tongues; to another the interpretation of tongues: 11 But all these worketh that one and the selfsame Spirit, dividing to every man severally as he will.

Little dove sings a new song

Psalm 33:3

3 Sing unto him a new song; play skilfully with a loud noise.

Psalm 40:3

3 And he hath put a new song in my mouth, even praise unto our God: many shall see it, and fear, and shall trust in the LORD.

Psalm 47:6

6 Sing praises to God, sing praises: sing praises unto our King, sing praises.

Psalm 66:1-2

1 Make a joyful noise unto God, all ye lands: 2 Sing forth the honour of his name: make his praise glorious.

Psalm 96:1-2

1 O sing unto the LORD a new song: sing unto the LORD, all the earth. 2 Sing unto the LORD, bless his name; shew forth his salvation from day to day.

Song of Songs 2:12

12 The flowers appear on the earth; the time of the singing of birds is come, and the voice of the turtle is heard in our land;

Galatians 4:6

6 And because ye are sons, God hath sent forth the Spirit of his Son into your hearts, crying, Abba, Father.

Ephesians 5:19-20

19 Speaking to yourselves in psalms and hymns and spiritual songs, singing and making melody in your heart to the Lord; 20 Giving thanks always for all things unto God and the Father in the name of our Lord Jesus Christ;

Flutters over the waters

Genesis 1:1-2

1 In the beginning God created the heaven and the earth. 2 And the earth was without form, and void; and darkness was upon the face of the deep. And the Spirit of God moved upon the face of the waters.

Job 26:13

13 By his spirit he hath garnished the heavens; his hand hath formed the crooked serpent.

Psalm 104:30

30 Thou sendest forth thy spirit, they are created: and thou renewest the face of the earth.

Lights gently

Isaiah 11:2

2 And the spirit of the LORD shall rest upon him, the spirit of wisdom and understanding, the spirit of counsel and might, the spirit of knowledge and of the fear of the LORD;

Matthew 3:16-17

16 And Jesus, when he was baptized, went up straightway out of the water: and, lo, the heavens were opened unto him, and he saw the Spirit of God descending like a dove, and lighting upon him: 17 And lo a voice from heaven, saying, This is my beloved Son, in whom I am well pleased.

John 1:32-34

32 And John bare record, saying, I saw the Spirit descending from heaven like a dove, and it abode upon him. 33 And I knew him not: but he that sent me to baptize with water, the same said unto me, Upon whom thou shalt see the Spirit descending, and remaining on him, the same is he which baptizeth with the Holy Ghost. 34 And I saw, and bare record that this is the Son of God.

Bathes in the light

John 16:13-15

13 Howbeit when he, the Spirit of truth, is come, he will guide you into all truth: for he shall not speak of himself; but whatsoever he shall hear, that shall he speak: and he will shew you things to come. 14 He shall glorify me: for he shall receive of mine, and shall shew it unto you. 15 All things that the Father hath are mine: therefore said I, that he shall take of mine, and shall shew it unto you.

Loves deeply

Song of Songs 5:12, 16b

12 His eyes are as the eyes of doves by the rivers of waters, washed with milk, and fitly set. 16b he is altogether lovely. This is my beloved, and this is my friend, O daughters of Jerusalem.

Romans 5:5b

5b because the love of God is shed abroad in our hearts by the Holy Ghost which is given unto us.

Romans 15:30

30 Now I beseech you, brethren, for the Lord Jesus Christ's sake, and for the love of the Spirit, that ye strive together with me in your prayers to God for me;

2 Corinthians 1:22

22 (God) Who hath also sealed us, and given the earnest of the Spirit in our hearts.

Quenches thirst

1 Corinthians 12:13

13 For by one Spirit are we all baptized into one body, whether we be Jews or Gentiles, whether we be bond or free; and have been all made to drink into one Spirit.

Breathes comforting coos

Genesis 2:7

7 And the LORD God formed man of the dust of the ground, and breathed into his nostrils the breath of life; and man became a living soul.

Job 33:4

4 The Spirit of God hath made me, and the breath of the Almighty hath given me life.

2 Samuel 23:2

2 The Spirit of the LORD spake by me, and his word was in my tongue.

Isaiah 40:7-8

7 The grass withereth, the flower fadeth: because the spirit of the LORD bloweth upon it: surely the people is grass. 8 The grass withereth, the flower fadeth: but the word of our God shall stand for ever.

Ezekiel 2:2

2 And the spirit entered into me when he spake unto me, and set me upon my feet, that I heard him that spake unto me.

John 14:16-17

16 And I will pray the Father, and he shall give you another Comforter, that he may abide with you for ever; 17 Even the Spirit of truth; whom the world cannot receive, because it seeth him not, neither knoweth him: but ye know him; for he dwelleth with you, and shall be in you.

John 20:22

22 And when he had said this, he breathed on them, and saith unto them, Receive ye the Holy Ghost:

Breathes comforting coos

Acts 9:31

31 Then had the churches rest throughout all Judaea and Galilee and Samaria, and were edified; and walking in the fear of the Lord, and in the comfort of the Holy Ghost, were multiplied.

1 Corinthians 3:16

16 Know ye not that ye are the temple of God, and that the Spirit of God dwelleth in you?

Galatians 4:6

6 And because ye are sons, God hath sent forth the Spirit of his Son into your hearts, crying, Abba, Father.

Hebrews 3:7

7 Wherefore (as the Holy Ghost saith, To day if ye will hear his voice,

Revelation 2:7

7 He that hath an ear, let him hear what the Spirit saith unto the churches; To him that overcometh will I give to eat of the tree of life, which is in the midst of the paradise of God.

Leads His flock

Exodus 33:14

14 And he said, My presence shall go with thee, and I will give thee rest.

Isaiah 63:14b

14b the Spirit of the LORD caused him to rest: so didst thou lead thy people, to make thyself a glorious name.

Luke 4:1

1 And Jesus being full of the Holy Ghost returned from Jordan, and was led by the Spirit into the wilderness,

Romans 8:14-16

14 For as many as are led by the Spirit of God, they are the sons of God. 15 For ye have not received the spirit of bondage again to fear; but ye have received the Spirit of adoption, whereby we cry, Abba, Father. 16 The Spirit itself beareth witness with our spirit, that we are the children of God:

Galatians 5:16a

16a This I say then, Walk in the Spirit,

Galatians 5:25

25 If we live in the Spirit, let us also walk in the Spirit.

Cries out in warning

Isaiah 59:19 (KJV)

19 So shall they fear the name of the LORD from the west, and his glory from the rising of the sun. When the enemy shall come in like a flood, the Spirit of the LORD shall lift up a standard against him.

1 Timothy 4:1

1 Now the Spirit speaketh expressly,

Cries out in warning

Judges 3:9-10a

9 And when the children of Israel cried unto the LORD, the LORD raised up a deliverer to the children of Israel, who delivered them, even Othniel the son of Kenaz, Caleb's younger brother. 10 And the Spirit of the LORD came upon him, and he judged Israel, and went out to war:

Judges 6:33-34

33 Then all the Midianites and the Amalekites and the children of the east were gathered together, and went over, and pitched in the valley of Jezreel. 34 But the Spirit of the LORD came upon Gideon, and he blew a trumpet; and Abiezer was gathered after him.

Flies freely and swiftly

Psalm 51:11-13

11 Cast me not away from thy presence; and take not thy holy spirit from me. 12 Restore unto me the joy of thy salvation; and uphold me with thy free spirit. 13 Then will I teach transgressors thy ways; and sinners shall be converted unto thee.

Romans 8:1-2

1 There is therefore now no condemnation to them which are in Christ Jesus, who walk not after the flesh, but after the Spirit. 2 For the law of the Spirit of life in Christ Jesus hath made me free from the law of sin and death.

2 Corinthians 3:17-18

17 Now the Lord is that Spirit: and where the Spirit of the Lord is, there is liberty. 18 But we all, with open face beholding as in a glass the glory of the Lord, are changed into the same image from glory to glory, even as by the Spirit of the Lord.

Teaches wisdom

Nehemiah 9:20a

20 Thou gavest also thy good spirit to instruct them

Isaiah 48:16-17

16 Come ye near unto me, hear ye this; I have not spoken in secret from the beginning; from the time that it was, there am I: and now the Lord GOD, and his Spirit, hath sent me. 17 Thus saith the LORD, thy Redeemer, the Holy One of Israel; I am the LORD thy God which teacheth thee to profit, which leadeth thee by the way that thou shouldest go.

John 14:26

26 But the Comforter, which is the Holy Ghost, whom the Father will send in my name, he shall teach you all things, and bring all things to your remembrance, whatsoever I have said unto you.

1 John 2:20

20 But ye have an unction from the Holy One, and ye know all things.

1 John 2:27

27 But the anointing which ye have received of him abideth in you, and ye need not that any man teach you: but as the same anointing teacheth you of all things, and is truth, and is no lie,

Crafts skillfully

Exodus 28:3

3 And thou shalt speak unto all that are wise hearted, whom I have filled with the spirit of wisdom, that they may make Aaron's garments to consecrate him, that he may minister unto me in the priest's office.

Exodus 31:1-6

1 And the LORD spake unto Moses, saying, 2 See, I have called by name Bezaleel the son of Uri, the son of Hur, of the tribe of Judah: 3 And I have filled him with the spirit of God, in wisdom, and in understanding, and in knowledge, and in all manner of workmanship, 4 To devise cunning works, to work in gold, and in silver, and in brass, 5 And in cutting of stones, to set them, and in carving of timber, to work in all manner of workmanship. 6 And I, behold, I have given with him Aholiab, the son of Ahisamach, of the tribe of Dan: and in the hearts of all that are wise hearted I have put wisdom, that they may make all that I have commanded thee;

Job 26:13

13 By his spirit he hath garnished the heavens; his hand hath formed the crooked serpent.

Psalm 104:30

30 Thou sendest forth thy spirit, they are created: and thou renewest the face of the earth.

Song of Songs 2:14

14 O my dove, that art in the clefts of the rock, in the secret places of the stairs, let me see thy countenance, let me hear thy voice; for sweet is thy voice, and thy countenance is comely.

Searches for good grain

Genesis 8:9-12

9 But the dove found no rest for the sole of her foot, and she returned unto him into the ark, for the waters were on the face of the whole earth: then he put forth his hand, and took her, and pulled her in unto him into the ark. 10 And he stayed yet other seven days; and again he sent forth the dove out of the ark; 11 And the dove came in to him in the evening; and, lo, in her mouth was an olive leaf pluckt off: so Noah knew that the waters were abated from off the earth. 12 And he stayed yet other seven days; and sent forth the dove; which returned not again unto him any more.

1 Corinthians 2:10-16

10 But God hath revealed them unto us by his Spirit: for the Spirit searcheth all things, yea, the deep things of God. 11 For what man knoweth the things of a man, save the spirit of man which is in him? even so the things of God knoweth no man, but the Spirit of God. 12 Now we have received, not the spirit of the world, but the spirit which is of God; that we might know the things that are freely given to us of God. 13 Which things also we speak, not in the words which man's wisdom teacheth, but which the Holy Ghost teacheth; comparing spiritual things with spiritual. 14 But the natural man receiveth not the things of the Spirit of God: for they are foolishness unto him: neither can he know them, because they are spiritually discerned. 15 But he that is spiritual judgeth all things, yet he himself is judged of no man. 16 For who hath known the mind of the Lord, that he may instruct him? But we have the mind of Christ.

Soars on mighty wings

Judges 14:5-6a

5 Then went Samson down, and his father and his mother, to Timnath, and came to the vineyards of Timnath: and, behold, a young lion roared against him. 6 And the Spirit of the LORD came mightily upon him, and he rent him as he would have rent a kid,

Micah 3:8

8 But truly I am full of power by the spirit of the LORD, and of judgment, and of might, to declare unto Jacob his transgression, and to Israel his sin.

Psalm 55:6

6 And I said, Oh that I had wings like a dove! for then would I fly away, and be at rest.

Psalm 68:13

13 Though ye have lien among the pots, yet shall ye be as the wings of a dove covered with silver, and her feathers with yellow gold.

Ecclesiastes 11:5

5 As thou knowest not what is the way of the spirit, nor how the bones do grow in the womb of her that is with child: even so thou knowest not the works of God who maketh all.

Acts 2:2-4

2 And suddenly there came a sound from heaven as of a rushing mighty wind, and it filled all the house where they were sitting. 3 And there appeared unto them cloven tongues like as of fire, and it sat upon each of them. 4 And they were all filled with the Holy Ghost, and began to speak with other tongues, as the Spirit gave them utterance.

Other acts of the Holy Spirit

Provides shelter

Psalm 61:1-4

1 Hear my cry, O God; attend unto my prayer. 2 From the end of the earth will I cry unto thee, when my heart is overwhelmed: lead me to the rock that is higher than I. 3 For thou hast been a shelter for me, and a strong tower from the enemy. 4 I will abide in thy tabernacle for ever: I will trust in the covert of thy wings. Selah.

Psalm 91:4-7

4 He shall cover thee with his feathers, and under his wings shalt thou trust: his truth shall be thy shield and buckler. 5 Thou shalt not be afraid for the terror by night; nor for the arrow that flieth by day; 6 Nor for the pestilence that walketh in darkness; nor for the destruction that wasteth at noonday. 7 A thousand shall fall at thy side, and ten thousand at thy right hand; but it shall not come nigh thee.

Prays on our behalf

Romans 8:26-27

26 Likewise the Spirit also helpeth our infirmities: for we know not what we should pray for as we ought: but the Spirit itself maketh intercession for us with groanings which cannot be uttered. 27 And he that searcheth the hearts knoweth what is the mind of the Spirit, because he maketh intercession for the saints according to the will of God.

Seals us

2 Corinthians 1:21-22

21 Now he which stablisheth us with you in Christ, and hath anointed us, is God; 22 Who hath also sealed us, and given the earnest of the Spirit in our hearts.

Ephesians 1:13-14

13 In whom ye also trusted, after that ye heard the word of truth, the gospel of your salvation: in whom also after that ye believed, ye were sealed with that holy Spirit of promise,14 Which is the earnest of our inheritance until the redemption of the purchased possession, unto the praise of his glory.

Ephesians 4:30-32

30 And grieve not the holy Spirit of God, whereby ye are sealed unto the day of redemption. 31 Let all bitterness, and wrath, and anger, and clamour, and evil speaking, be put away from you, with all malice: 32 And be ye kind one to another, tenderhearted, forgiving one another, even as God for Christ's sake hath forgiven you.

2 Timothy 2:19a

19 Nevertheless the foundation of God standeth sure, having this seal, The Lord knoweth them that are his.

Sorrows

Isaiah 38:14

14 Like a crane or a swallow, so did I chatter: I did mourn as a dove: mine eyes fail with looking upward: O LORD, I am oppressed; undertake for me.

Anoints and brings joy and peace

Psalm 23:5
5 Thou preparest a table before me in the presence of mine enemies: thou anointest my head with oil; my cup runneth over.

Mark 6:12-13
12 And they went out, and preached that men should repent.
13 And they cast out many devils, and anointed with oil many that were sick, and healed them.

Luke 4:18
18 The Spirit of the Lord is upon me, because he hath anointed me to preach the gospel to the poor; he hath sent me to heal the brokenhearted, to preach deliverance to the captives, and recovering of sight to the blind, to set at liberty them that are bruised,

Acts 10:38
38 How God anointed Jesus of Nazareth with the Holy Ghost and with power: who went about doing good, and healing all that were oppressed of the devil; for God was with him.

Romans 14:17
17 For the kingdom of God is not meat and drink; but righteousness, and peace, and joy in the Holy Ghost.

Galatians 5:22
22 But the fruit of the Spirit is love, joy, peace, longsuffering, gentleness, goodness, faith,

1 Thessalonians 1:6
6 And ye became followers of us, and of the Lord, having received the word in much affliction, with joy of the Holy Ghost:

Matthew 10:16
16 Behold, I send you forth as sheep in the midst of wolves: be ye therefore wise as serpents, and harmless as doves.

Further explanation and ideas:

1. Your child does not need to fully understand the concept of the Trinity in order to grasp the basic concept that God is the Father, Jesus is the Son, and the Holy Spirit is the third person member sent to live within each of His believers. What is paramount is that they are aware that the Holy Spirit never leaves us. He is with us from the instant that we accept Christ into our lives. I recommend that it become a practice to look for references to the Spirit each time you and your child read scripture. He is there in The Word just as He has always existed from eternity past throughout eternity future.

2. The concepts of growth and change are important in understanding how the Holy Spirit works. Before either can occur, there must be the initial infilling. The concept of the "new song" represents the moment that we are set apart for the Lord. Engage your child in discussion regarding the newness which starts the change which leads us to be more like God would have us. The scriptures call it going from glory to glory.

3. The great thing about the discussion of the Holy Spirit is that His movement produces action. Fluttering over water can be demonstrated by stirring your finger through a bowl of water, skipping rocks across a body of water, or by blowing over water. The important observation is that the action of the Spirit causes movement on the water. Our lives are like the water. We become stirred up, producing change in our lives. The movement creates a rippling and desire to change.

4. As the Spirit lights upon us, He brings peace. He lands ever so gently, sitting with us, calming our fears and removing anxiety. It has the effect of a giant hug from heaven. Your child might understand it if you say that the Holy Spirit comes to hold their hand.

5. When the light from the sun shines on our bodies, we feel the warmth it brings. It is similar with heavenly light. The Holy Spirit directs our thoughts and prayers to God through Jesus. The Spirit is our connection to heaven.

6. As we allow the Spirit to fill us each day, He will cause us to be more and more loving. We will love our family and friends better. We will truly love God and Jesus.

7. Just like people thirst for water, Christians thirst to learn more about God's word and will for their lives. The Holy Spirit quenches this thirst by filling us daily with His gifts.

8. Although we do not hear His voice, the Spirit speaks to us in ways that we hear with our heart. We need to allow Him to guide us. He will always give us the best instruction.

9. We are told to "walk in the Spirit." This means to seek His guidance. He will lead us individually, as a family, a church, and a nation. Just follow.

10. When danger is in our path, the Spirit will let us know. Like a screeching dove, He will sound a warning. Listen with your heart when you sense trouble.

11. The Spirit keeps us free from bondage. Sometimes we get ourselves all tied up with things that we should not. Lies, bad choices, addictions, and wrongdoings will cause our lives to be trapped in places that are not the best. If we are listening to the Spirit, we will not go there.

12. We should desire the wisdom that comes from the Holy Spirit. Wisdom will set our feet on the right path. It will cause us to make good decisions.

13. Our talents come from God. He has given us the Spirit so that we can put our skills to use for His kingdom. The Spirit was present when the earth was created. He was there when we were created. He helps us to build and create.

14. The Holy Spirit will help us find the good things in life. He wants us to have the best that God has to offer. He will also help us to desire what is best.

15. There is mighty power in the Spirit of The Lord. We are weak, but He is strong. His wings will help us soar and not be weary. Your child can learn to rely on Him to carry them through life.

16. Encourage your child to study the individual pictures of the little dove and have them describe the actions of the dove. Although the dove is behaving like a bird, his actions represent those of the Holy Spirit. Using your knowledge of the Holy Spirit, point out how the actions mirror His spiritual activity.

17. Have your child identify times throughout their day that the Spirit was working in and through them. For example, they might have had a decision to make that was aided by the power of the Holy Spirit.

18. Help your child make a list of areas where they might pray for the Holy Spirit to strengthen and guide them. Talk about the actions of the Holy Spirit which will help them achieve these things. Perhaps they want to learn to play a musical instrument and they need skill. They may have trouble starting a new task and they need stirring. After a few days or weeks you can review the list together and praise God for the help of the Holy Spirit.

Notes and Thoughts

Notes and Thoughts

Bibliography

Dake, Finis J. The KJV Dake Annotated Reference Bible. Lawrenceville, Georgia: Dake Bible Publishers, 1963.

Holy Bible: King James Version WORDsearch CROSS e-book.

Lockyer, Herbert. All the Doctrine's of The Bible. Grand Rapids, Michigan: Zondervan, 1964.

Made in the USA
Charleston, SC
20 March 2015